THE
BALFOUR VISIT

**HOW AMERICA RECEIVED HER
DISTINGUISHED GUEST; AND THE
SIGNIFICANCE OF THE CONFERENCES
IN THE UNITED STATES IN 1917**

EDITED BY

CHARLES HANSON TOWNE

NEW YORK
GEORGE H. DORAN COMPANY

THE BALFOUR VISIT *91*

CHARLES HANSON TOWNE

THE RIGHT HON. A. J. BALFOUR, O.M., M.P.
Head of the Mission.
Some time Prime Minister of the United Kingdom of
Great Britain and Ireland.

CONTENTS

CONTENTS

ILLUSTRATIONS

THE BALFOUR VISIT

THE BALFOUR VISIT

GREAT BRITAIN could not have made a happier choice in the man who represented her in the United States immediately after America entered the Great War.

The Right Honourable Arthur James Balfour, M. P., O. M., bears a name known and revered on both sides of the Atlantic. His coming was hailed as a great event. His dignity, his poise, his tact, his vast experience in diplomatic affairs, his success as a speaker, both as to manner and matter, his age—everything was in his favour. We Americans were well aware of his long and wonderful career in England. We had not forgotten the splendid work he had done as Prime Minister, when, in 1902, he succeeded Lord Salisbury. We had not forgotten his significant pamphlet on "Insular Free Trade;" and we recalled how, in 1904, when the Russian-Japanese War seemed certain to cause serious complications in England, Balfour, with infinite patience and tact, tided over and smoothed out the unhappy incident of the firing by the Russian Baltic fleet on the English fishing fleet in the North Sea. We likewise remembered that his institution of the permanent Committee of Imperial Defence, and of the New Army Council, during the same year, were movements of the greatest significance and importance. Then, too, we knew Mr. Balfour not only as a statesman of the rarest gifts, but as a writer of many notable volumes, a student, a profound thinker, a man who might easily have made his mark as a philosopher if diplomatic life had not called him more insistently.

The United States entered this tremendous conflict early in April, 1917, and instantly both the British and French governments decided to send to our shores an extraordinary commission, the purpose of which would be the expression of the appreciation of our stand. This commission was, among other things, to discuss with us how best we might serve the Allied nations already at war, and to learn how they could secure our most effective co-operation in the struggle. For things had to be done, and quickly. Each day's delay was dangerous, and England, in particular, did not wish us to repeat her errors, so tragic in their results. Her friendly hand reached us from across the sea; and we clasped it when we greeted Balfour.

BALFOUR'S TACT

Mr. Balfour came to this country deeply conscious of America's susceptibilities and sensitivenesses, deeply aware, too, of the irritation aroused by the protests of two and a half years of neutrality and of feeling that was chronically anti-British. That the mission succeeded at all is due to a breadth of vision on Mr. Balfour's part which will rank as one of the cardinal points of Anglo-American relations, and to as finely developed and executed a publicity system as it is possible to imagine.

From Mr. Balfour down to the humblest member of the mission ran the constant statement that the British had come to serve, not to interfere; to offer the fruits of their own bitter experiences, not to lay down for us what we should do. Never once did a member of the mission make himself obtrusive or officious; never once was the lesson taught by the master mind at the head forgotten.

None of the mission presumed to advise what the United States should do. Instead, all of them met questions somewhat in this way: "Well, in England we were faced with somewhat similar conditions and came to such and such a decision. Now this decision worked out so and so." The American could take it or leave it; there was no obligation on either side. Nevertheless, as one would predict, he most often chose to take it.

Of course the most difficult part of the mission was its presentation to the American public in such a way as to stir interest and enthusiasm and prevent any possible unpleasantness from the newness and unexpectedness of the Alliance. Mr. Balfour himself was a master in this art, both in the magnetism of his appearance and in the warmth and appropriateness of his speeches. Obviously, however, he was too occupied to prepare a detailed publicity campaign.

This work he entrusted to Mr. Geoffrey Butler, who had formerly handled American news at the Foreign Office. He met the correspondents twice daily to outline the work of the mission, discuss special subjects, and arrange individual interviews. He found the press voracious and he satisfied it. He first suggested to Mr. Balfour that he should address all the correspondents; then that General Bridges speak of the evils of the voluntary system; Admiral de Chair of submarines; Major Rees of aeroplanes; Sir Hartman Lever of finance; Mr. Anderson of wheat; Mr. Amos of the British priority system; Lord Eustace Percy of shipping; Mr. Malcolm of Red Cross work and the identification of the dead. Finally Mr. Balfour in farewell addressed the National Press Club.

These interviews were not perfunctory. Each official told his story, after which the correspondents, varying from fifteen to one hundred, were free to draw him out on any line desired. The press, keen and eager, new to the war, drew upon the Britishers' experiences with avidity and flooded the wires with fascinating stories for the newest belligerent people. That so many officials spoke with such freedom as they did is an undying tribute to the spirit with which Mr. Balfour had pervaded the mission and to the relations which were at once established with the press.

Strangely enough, it was the first of such interviews, that with General Bridges, which for a brief nervous time threatened an explosion. The General, a huge, strapping soldier who had never made a speech in his life and who did not know how to mince words, came out flatly against the voluntary system at a time when a sensitive and susceptible Congress was wrestling with that fundamental subject. General Bridges, speaking only of England's experience, shot that system into a thousand fallacies which flared out from every newspaper heading almost before the words were cold.

Every one's breath was held to see what Congress would do. Spectres rose of anti-British speeches, interference with the prerogatives of the legislature, etc., but by good fortune there was so much vital meat in what the General had said and so much of a cry of anguish from those of England who had suffered under the voluntary system that Congress spent all its time reading the good sense he had uttered instead of criticising the policy behind his utterance. And then they voted for conscription.

The success of this first interview set the pace for the others, and one expert after another told his story to the press with a confidence that all were working to the same end. None of the others, as it happened, was on such hair-trigger subjects as General Bridges', but they were none the less interesting. Just how much educational material went out from Washington because of this liberal publicity policy it is impossible even to approximate; but certain it is that it opened a new era of friendliness between the two countries.

The mission was forced on its first arrival to waste considerable time, as most of its experts could, naturally enough, find no corresponding officials in the American government with whom to negotiate. It had come to this country as a complete war organism, equipped with experts in many lines; such as a wheat commissioner, a priority expert, a trade regulator, and other specialists, who at once made evident the gaps in America's war organisation. The needs of peace had not developed powerful bureaus to meet the necessities which two and a half years of war

had shown to exist in Europe, but every moment
wasted had its recompense in suggestiveness to
this country. Probably in no other way would
America's needs have been illuminated more
quickly and constructively.

THE ARRIVAL OF THE MISSION

It was on April eleventh that the British Commissioners embarked on a fast ship, and secretly
began the voyage to America. There was, of
course, great danger of German spies; but every
precaution was taken, and no untoward incident
marred the trip. A close watch was kept for the
ubiquitous submarine; but, fortunately, no peri-
scope appeared; and, after an uneventful journey,
the Commission touched shore at Halifax on
April twentieth. They immediately crossed to
St. John, where a train awaited them and took
them to the tiny village of McAdam, just beyond
the International Bridge. This is the structure,
most people will remember, that Werner Horn,
formerly a German officer, tried to wreck with
dynamite.

The Foreign Minister and former Premier's
personal staff included such celebrities as the
Hon. Sir Eric Drummond, K. C. M. G., C. B.;
Ian Malcolm, M. P.; Cecil Dormer, and Geoffrey
Butler. Sir Eric Drummond is a brother-in-law
of the late Duke of Norfolk, and a prominent

Roman Catholic layman; but perhaps the most interesting thing about him is the fact that he has been private secretary (in England this is equivalent more or less to assistant) to Mr. Asquith, Sir E. Grey and Mr. Balfour. This has probably given him as much insight into the affairs of Europe as any man now serving in the public interests.

Mr. Malcolm has been, at various times, an *attaché* of the British Embassies in Petrograd, Berlin, and Paris, and, during the present conflict, he has been the British Red Cross Officer in Russia, Switzerland, and France.

The other members of the distinguished party included Lieutenant General T. M. Bridges, C. M. G., D. S. O.; Captain H. H. Spender-Clay, M. P.; Rear Admiral Sir Dudley R. S. de Chair, K. C. B., M. V. O.; Fleet Paymaster Vincent Lawford, D. S. O., Admiralty, and Lord Cunliffe, Governor of the Bank of England. Captain Spender-Clay, it will be recalled, married the daughter of William Waldorf Astor.

The Commission also included the following:

War Office.—Colonel Goodwin, Colonel Langhorne, Major L. W. B. Rees, V. C., M. C., Royal Flying Corps, and Major C. E. Dansey.

Blockade Department Experts.—Lord Eustace Percy, of the Foreign Office; A. A. Paton, of the Foreign Office; F. P. Robinson, of the Board of Trade; S. McKenna, of the War Trade Intelligence Department, and M. D. Peterson of the Foreign Trade Department, Foreign Office.

Wheat Commission.—A. A. Anderson, Chairman, and Mr. Vigor.

Munitions.—W. T. Layton, Director of Requirements and Statistics Branch, Secretariat of the Ministry of Munitions; C. T. Phillips, American and Transport Department, Ministry of Munitions; Captain Leeming, Mr. Amos.

Ordnance and Lines of Communication.—Captain Heron.

Supplies and Transports.—Major Puckle.

It may not be amiss to tell here, with the special permission of Mr. Frederic Coleman, who wrote that interesting book, "From Mons to Ypres with General French," the following story of one member of the Balfour party who is greatly loved. I refer to Lieutenant General Bridges. Here is the tale:

Major, now Lieutenant General, Tom Bridges, of the Fourth Dragoon Guards, had been sent into St. Quentin on Friday afternoon to see if more stragglers could be found. In the square near the Mairie he found a couple of hundred or more men of various detachments, who were seated on the pavement in complete exhaustion and utter resignation to what appeared their inability to rejoin the army, which had retreated far to the southward.

They, too, expected the Germans momentarily.

A couple of half-crazed, irresponsible chaps had preached some rot to them that made them think themselves abandoned to their fate. Bridges needed but a moment to see how far gone they were, how utterly and hopelessly fatigued. No peremptory order, no gentle request, no clever cajolery would suffice. With most of them the power to move seemed to have gone with ceaseless tramping, without food or sleep, for the thirty-six hours past.

A brilliant idea came to the big, genial Major. Entering a toy shop, he bought a toy drum and a penny whistle. He strapped the little drum to his belt.

"Can you play 'The British Grenadiers'?" he asked his trumpeter.

"Sure, sir," was the reply.

In a twinkling the pair were marching round the square, the high treble of the tiny toy whistle rising clear and shrill. "But of all the world's brave heroes, There's none that can compare, With a tow, row, row, with a tow, row, row, To the British Grenadiers."

Round they came, the trumpeter, caught on the wings of the Major's enthusiasm, putting his very heart and soul into every inspiring note.

Bridges, supplying the comic relief with the small sticks in his big hands, banged away on the drum like mad.

They reached the recumbent group. They passed its tired length. Now they came to the last man. Will they feel the spirit of the straining notes, rich with the tradition of the grand old air? Will they catch the spirit of the big-hearted Major, who knows so well just how the poor lads feel, and seeks that spot of humour in Tommy's make-up that has so often proved his very salvation? The spark has caught! Some with tears in their eyes, some with a roar of laughter, jump to their feet and fall in. The weary feet, sore and bruised, tramp the hard cobbles unconscious of their pain. Stiffened limbs answer to call of newly awakened wills.

"With a tow, row, row, with a tow, row, row, to the British Grenadiers." They are singing it now as they file in long column down the street after the big form hammering the toy drum, and his panting trumpeter "blowing his head off" beside him.

"Go on, Colonel! We'll follow you to hell," sings out a brawny Irishman behind who can just hobble along on his torn feet.

Never a man of all the lot was left behind.

Down the road, across the bridge, mile after mile towards Roye. The trumpeter, blown, subsides for a while, then, refreshed, takes up the burden of the noble tune again.

At last Tom Bridges turned and said: "Now,

boys, ahead of you is a town where you can get food and drink and a bit of rest before you go on. It isn't far. Good luck!"

But not they. They were not going to lose their new-found patron. Clamour rose, shrill and eager. "Don't leave us, Colonel," they begged. "Don't, for God's sake, leave us! They all left us but you. We'll follow you anywhere, but where to go when you leave we don't know at all."

So Bridges toiled on to Roye with them, got them food and billets, turned them over to some one who would see they got on to their commands in some way, and went back to duty with his regiment, arriving at two o'clock in the morning.

Big Tom Bridges! Indeed, he had more than once earned the name, but never more gallantly and wisely than on that afternoon in August in the turmoil of the great retreat.

While the British Commission was still on the Canadian border, the American Reception Committee quietly left Washington on April fifteenth. It was headed by Breckinridge Long, who is Third Assistant Secretary of State; Rear Admiral Fletcher, and Major General Leonard Wood, with Colonel Mackie, also on the Root Commission in Russia. They were given to understand that the British party had left two days earlier than it had, and they waited with anxiety from Monday until Friday afternoon, when a message from Halifax relieved their vigil, and caused them to press on to the border in a flight by night. Arriving at the tiny frontier town of Vanceboro, Maine, on the twenty-first, the American party, together with the army and navy representatives in full uniform, descended to a dilapidated station platform, the forlornest place one could imagine. To add to their troubles, the spot was enveloped by a cold mist, so thick that it could be cut with a knife. Of course, in some mysterious way, the fact had leaked out that such distinguished guests were expected in this out-of-the-way place, and a conglomerate crowd quickly gathered, made up of French Canadians, railway workers, farmers, and a few little children, the latter proudly bearing three tattered American flags.

It was in such surroundings that the great British Commission received its formal greeting on American soil. There was no fanfare of trumpets, no beating of drums, no sounding of brass and cymbals: just a quiet, homely reception on the part of Secretary Long after the special train had crossed the bridge.

BALFOUR'S FIRST WORDS

The Commission was due to arrive in Washington at three o'clock on Sunday afternoon,

April twenty-second. Just after leaving Vanceboro, in the dining-car, in time to reach the Sunday papers, Mr. Balfour was induced to make a
statement to one or two special correspondents;
and his first words were these:

All will agree that my first duty as head of a diplomatic mission is to pay my respects to the head of the
State to which I have been sent, and no public expression of opinion on points of policy would, I think, be
useful or even tolerable until I have had the honour of
conferring with your President and learning his views.
I have not come here to make speeches or indulge in
interviews, but to do what I can to make co-operation
easy and effective between those who are striving with
all their power to bring about a lasting peace by the
only means that can secure it; namely, a successful
war.

Without, however, violating the rule I have just laid
down, there are two things which I may permit myself to say: one on my own behalf, the other on behalf of my countrymen in general.

On my own behalf, let me express the deep gratification I feel at being connected in any capacity whatever
with events which associate our countries in a common
effort for a great ideal.

On behalf of my countrymen, let me express our
gratitude for all that the citizens of the United States
of America have done to mitigate the lot of those who,
in the allied countries, have suffered from the cruelties
of the most deliberately cruel of all wars. To name no
others, the efforts of Mr. Gerard to alleviate the condition of British and other prisoners of war in Germany,

and the administrative genius which Mr. Hoover has
ungrudgingly devoted to the relief of the unhappy
Belgians and French in the territories still in enemy
occupation, will never be forgotten, while an inexhaust-
ible stream of charitable effort has supplied medical
and nursing skill to the service of the wounded and
the sick.

These are the memorable doings of a beneficent neutrality. But the days of neutrality are, I rejoice to
think, at an end, and the first page is being turned in
a new chapter in the history of mankind.

Your President, in a most apt and vivid phrase, has
proclaimed that the world must be made safe for democracy. Democracies, wherever they are to be found,
and not least the democracies of the British Empire,
will hail the pronouncement as a happy augury.

That self-governing communities are not to be
treated as negligible simply because they are small,
that the ruthless domination of one unscrupulous
power imperils the future of civilisation and the liber-
ties of mankind, are truths of political ethics which
the bitter experiences of war are burning into the souls
of all freedom-loving peoples. That this great people should have thrown themselves whole-heartedly
into this mighty struggle, prepared for all the efforts
and sacrifices that may be required to win success for
this most righteous cause, is an event at once so happy
and so momentous that only the historian of the future
will be able, as I believe, to measure its true proportions.

The manuscript (in Mr. Balfour's handwriting) of this, his first utterance on United States

soil, is preserved in the Library of Princeton University.

This speech was written by Mr. Balfour the night before he landed, sitting up late into the night in his cabin. It was substituted for a version previously written and rejected at the eleventh hour on later consideration. Mr. Balfour never dictates. Everything is written in long hand and carefully revised.

In this first utterance the trained diplomat was revealed, the man who knew his ground, who recognised his responsibilities. England must have been proud of this initial expression of her representative; as America was proud to receive it.

THE RECEPTION IN WASHINGTON

Secretary of State Lansing, accompanied by Colonel W. W. Harts, the President's Aid; Frank L. Polk, Counsellor of the State Department and Assistant Secretary of State; Sir Cecil Spring-Rice, the British Ambassador; and several others equally notable, met the party when it arrived at the station in Washington. Two cavalry troops were likewise on hand, as a special escort, and the visitors were at once taken to the private residence of Franklin MacVeagh, former Secretary of the Treasury. Mr. MacVeagh had graciously put his house at their disposal.

We Americans like distinguished visitors, and we make the most of them. If one comes with the right credentials, there is always a warm welcome awaiting him. There are cheers all along the line of march after his ship comes in, and weeks of veritable holiday-making for any authentic representative of a friendly nation. Certainly Mr. Balfour had no reason to complain of the reception which greeted him in Washington that first day. The streets and avenues were crowded with people anxious to pay him tribute, to bid him welcome. Everywhere cheers, and—a novel experience—the hooting of motor horns. And everywhere flags and banners, for at last the Stars and Stripes could be displayed with the Union Jack. Our technical neutrality was over. There were no more fears. The die had been cast. And the people of America have seldom been happier. They were proud with an understandable pride; and their eagerness to express their elation was almost pathetic. No one minded his tears; they were tears of joy—joy in a common cause, the cause of humanity and righteousness.

As one looks back now, it is easy to understand that there may have been a little confusion on the part of the Entente Powers concerning our attitude with regard to Germany. The Allies never had any misconception as to our stand on

Prussian militarism, but they might have been justified in the belief that our policy and theirs, when it touched upon trade regulations, the treatment of neutrals, and plans for world reconstruction after the war, would differ. Balfour's visit was made in order that these and kindred subjects should be brought out into the light; that we might get together amicably and swiftly, and crush once and for all the foul German propaganda that seemed to be forever in the air. Mr. Balfour was the driving force and actual chairman of all the committees in which the mission worked. In his brain their work was all co-ordinated and divergencies of aim smoothed over.

Balfour and Lansing were photographed together, and the picture, now famous, went the rounds of the press.

THE FIRST MEETING WITH THE PRESIDENT

On the morning of April twenty-third the British Foreign Minister had his first interview with President Wilson; and that same evening the President and Mrs. Wilson gave a large dinner at the White House in honour of the party. Here, perhaps, was formed in Mr. Balfour's mind that profound sentiment of admiration for President Wilson of which, since he has returned, he has made no secret.

It must be remembered that the French Commission was also here at the same time; and while Mr. Balfour was being greeted everywhere by the populace, General Joffre and M. Viviani were likewise being acclaimed. These were thrilling days in the Capitol. Events crowded on top of one another thick and fast, and the public was more than satisfied that the right representatives had been sent from both England and France.

There is a pretty story told of Mr. Balfour's meeting the French Commission, standing, bareheaded, on the seat of a motor, backed into the crowd just outside the French Mission's house. The sight of the tall figure with the grey locks brought Viviani to his feet with a waving of his hat and a courteous, sweeping bow.

SEEKING NO FORMAL ALLIANCE

It was on April twenty-fifth that Mr. Balfour, facing a semicircle of perhaps fifty correspondents in a beautiful room of the MacVeagh home, gave his first talk. The press had not expected a speech, and only the forethought of the representative of the Chicago *Tribune,* who had provided a stenographer, preserved this speech intact. This is what Mr. Balfour said:

I do not suppose that it is possible for you—I am sure it would not be possible for me were I in your place—to realise in concrete detail all that the war

means to those who have been engaged in it for now
two years and a half. That is a feeling which comes,
and can only come, by actual experience. We on the
other side of the Atlantic have been living in an at-
mosphere of war since August, 1914, and you cannot
move about the streets, you cannot go about your daily
business, even if your affairs be dissociated with the
war itself, without having evidences of the war brought
to your notice every moment.

I arrived here on Sunday afternoon and went out
in the evening after dark, and I was struck by a somewhat unusual feeling which at the first moment I did
not analyse; and suddenly it came upon me that this
was the first time for two years and a half or more
when I had seen a properly lighted street. There is
not a street in London, there is not a street in any
city in the United Kingdom in which after dark the
whole community is not wrapped in a gloom exceed-
ing that which must have existed before the invention
of gas or electric lighting. But that is a small matter,
and I mention it only because it happened to strike
me as one of my earliest experiences in this city.

Of course, the more tragic side of war is never, and
cannot ever be, absent from our minds. I saw with
great regret this morning in the newspapers that the
son of Bonar Law, our Chancellor of the Exchequer,
was wounded and missing in some of the operations
now going on in Palestine, and I instinctively cast my
mind back to the losses of this war in all circles, but
as an illustration it seems to me impressive. I went
over the melancholy list, and, if my memory serves
me right, out of the small number of Cabinet
Ministers, men of Cabinet rank who were serving the
State when the war broke out in August, 1914, one

nas been killed in action, four at least have lost sons. That is the sort of things that have happened in quite a small and narrowly restricted class of men, but it is characteristic of what is happening throughout the whole country.

The condition of France in that respect is evidently even more full of sorrow and tragedy than our own. because we had not a great army; we had but a small army when war broke out, whereas the French Army was of the great Continental type, was on a war footing, and was, from the very inception of military operations, engaged in sanguinary conflict with the common enemy.

We have to-day among us a mission from France. I doubt not—indeed, I am fully convinced—that they will receive a welcome not less warm, not less heartfelt, than that which you have so generously and encouragingly extended to us. That was, and certainly will be, increased by the reflection that one member of the mission is Marshal Joffre, who will go down through all time as the general in command of the allied forces at one of the most critical moments in the world's history.

I remember when I was here before there was a book which was given as a prize in the schools called "The Fifteen Decisive Battles of the World." I do not know whether they all quite deserve that title, but there can be no doubt or question whatever that among the decisive battles of the world the Battle of the Marne was the most decisive. It was a turning point in the history of mankind, and I rejoice that the hero of that event is to-day coming among us and will join us, the British Nation, in laying before the people of the United States our gratitude for the sym-

pathy which they have shown and are showing, and
our warm confidence in the value of the assistance
which they are affording the allied cause.

Gentlemen, I do not believe that the magnitude of
that assistance can by any possibility be exaggerated.
I am told that there are some doubting critics who
seem to think that the object of the mission of France
and Great Britain to this country is to inveigle the
United States out of its traditional policy and to en-
tangle it in formal alliances, secret or public, with
European powers. I cannot imagine any rumour with
less foundation, nor can I imagine a policy so utterly
unnecessary.

Our confidence in the assistance which we are going
to get from this community is not based upon such
shallow considerations as those which arise out of
formal treaties. No treaty could increase the un-
doubted confidence with which we look to the United
States, who, having come into the war, are going to
see the war through. . . . I feel perfectly certain that
you will throw into it all your unequalled resources,
all your powers of invention, of production, all your
man power, all the resources of that country which
has greater resources than any other country in the
world; and, already having come to the decision, nothing will turn you from it but success crowning our
joint efforts.

THE GREAT DAY AT MT. VERNON

When the French Commission visited the tomb
of Washington at Mount Vernon on April
twenty-ninth, a card attached to a wonderful

wreath of lilies was placed beside a bronze palm which Marshal Joffre had laid on the marble sarcophagus. On this card, in Mr. Balfour's own handwriting, were these beautiful words:

"Dedicated by the British Mission to the immortal memory of George Washington, soldier, statesman, patriot, who would have rejoiced to see the country of which he was by birth a citizen, and the country his genius called into existence, fighting side by side to save mankind from a military despotism."

What greater tribute could he have paid the noble Washington?

The day, which had been lowering and heavy as the official party glided down the Potomac on the Presidential Yacht *Mayflower,* and had even threatened rain as every one stood at attention at "Taps" opposite the historic mansion, suddenly broke into the promise of full sunshine as the half hundred spectators wound their way up to the silent sarcophagus. The foliage was rich in its spring newness and the three Allied flags, British, French, and American, lent another touch of colour as they flew proudly over the grave.

After M. Viviani had delivered an impassioned speech, Secretary Daniels beckoned Mr. Balfour forward without introduction. The British Foreign Secretary advanced slowly be-

fore the open sarcophagus, bare-headed and evidently deeply touched. Standing beneath his own
flag, before the tomb of the man who tore the
richest jewel from the British crown, with the
sunlight playing through the cedar trees upon his
finely chiselled features, he spoke slowly, feel-
ingly, amidst a silence sacred to the scene.

My friend and colleague, M. Viviani, in phrases
burning with emotion, and in eloquent language, not
only has paid tribute to the hero who is buried here,
but has brought our thoughts down to the present
crisis, the greatest in the world's history. He has
told us of the people of France, England, Belgium,
Russia, Italy, and Serbia who have sacrificed their
lives for what they believe to be the cause of liberty.
No spot on the face of the earth, where a speech in
behalf of liberty might be made, could be more appro-
priate than the tomb of Washington.

Then came Marshal Joffre, with a brief but
glowing tribute; and Mr. Balfour and General
Bridges, Great Britain's chief army representative in the mission, placed a British wreath above
the tomb. Happily, then, the three flags of Great
Britain, France, and the United States were
rested upon it. A momentous occasion indeed, a
day that will go down in history. For we were
the allies at last of England and France! And
here was concrete expression of the great truth.
The handful of people who were privileged to

IAN MALCOLM, ESQ., M.P.
Parliamentary Private Secretary to Mr. Balfour.
Red Cross Representative with the Mission.

witness that scene were almost awed by its significance. None of them, it is safe to say, will ever forget it. And as Mr. Balfour and his fellow missioners strolled about the spacious Mt. Vernon lawns afterwards and inspected every detail of the home with deep interest, the feeling of consecration still endured.

BALFOUR'S HUMANITY

Of course there were amusing incidents during Mr. Balfour's visit. He endeared himself to the people when they learned how democratic he was; how he tried on several occasions to escape from the restraints of the diplomatic net. There is nothing that the American people like quite so well as that. A story went the rounds as to how, one day, when Mr. Balfour was invited to lunch with a friend of many years' standing, Mr. Henry White, he sought to evade the motor that was waiting at the door to conduct him. He slipped out of a side entrance, so that he might walk alone and in peace to the home of his friend. It was only a few squares, anyhow. Even the Scotland Yard man who had accompanied him to America, was not aware that his distinguished charge had vanished until some time afterwards. Like royalty, Mr. Balfour was "found out"; and to his sorrow the occasion never presented itself again when he could repeat such a human escapade.

Again, the American people were delighted with Mr. Balfour when they learned that he loved to read "penny dreadfuls." His delight in golf they could understand; indeed, they expected that: but to find that so great a personage actually lost himself in tales like "The Stain on the Staircase" and "The Man With the Missing Toe" tickled their hearts. He was not a high-brow, after all! But even if he was, he was the right kind of high-brow. And when he couldn't remember the names of the authors of his favourite shockers, but confessed this an example of human ingratitude, the people loved him all over again. He was so human, and he "made no bones," as we say, about admitting his weaknesses. It was all along the line that Balfour came—and conquered.

He even conquered—sometimes—when he played tennis with Secretary McAdoo and Counsellor Polk, and others. And he won the hearts of the newspaper men when he announced that the press would be received twice daily in the Hotel Shoreham, not up-town; another example of his thoughtfulness.

Mr. Balfour dispelled a rather general but absurd misconception held on each side of the Atlantic. He showed America, for instance, that

Great Britain's greatest statesmen are often
merely "Mr." He showed England, as Lord
Eustace Percy pointed out, that it was not necessary to send a wild man to this country.

GETTING DOWN TO WORK

It was soon after the discovery of these human
traits in the great statesman that an informal
conference was held at the Balfour headquarters.
Only members of the British party and of the
staff of the British Embassy were permitted to
be present. The talk, it became known, was of
a most general kind; the chief desire was to get
down to work, to organise some plan so that the
mission could effectively handle affairs as they
came up; but this could not be done, it was agreed,
until the actual arrival of the French diplomats.
Both the British and the French wished to co-
ordinate and to work in the closest harmony.

At the Pan-American Union Building a reception was held on the evening of the same day
(April twenty-fourth), so that Mr. Balfour and
his *confrères* could meet certain members of Congress and other Government officials whom they
might not see again in the course of their regular
work. Secretary Lansing stood at the head of
the receiving line. Several dinners had been
given, previous to the reception, at the homes of
various Secretaries. Mr. Lansing, Mr. Baker,

Mr. Daniels and Mr. McAdoo were among those who entertained.

It was understood that Mr. Balfour would present, not so much the British questions involved, as a whole picture of the problems confronting the Entente Alliance. As one newspaper wisely pointed out, "England has very largely supplied some of her Allies with both finance and shipping, and it is impossible to go into her financial or shipping situation without examining their reflex on the other co-operating nations."

ENTERTAINING THE MISSION

Socially, as befitted their position, the mission was lionised. Mr. Balfour, besides his formal call and dinner with President Wilson, dined privately at the White House twice and met the President on several other occasions for important negotiations. The two statesmen are uncommonly alike, in their intellectuality, their rather cloistered lives, and their manner of approach.

Mr. Balfour dined also with Secretary Lansing and the other cabinet members, and was tendered two large official receptions, one by Secretary Lansing, and the other by Ambassador Spring-Rice at the British Embassy. Beyond that he was entertained by many former friends and well-known Washingtonians.

The other members of the mission, apart from their work, found time for considerable personal pleasure. Rear Admiral Sir Dudley R. S. de Chair was tendered a very formal reception, in the name of the British Navy, by the Navy League of the United States; and, later, signalised the joy of his Navy at having American destroyers in British waters, by laying a wreath on Admiral Dewey's tomb. General Bridges addressed a large gathering of publishers in New York, and Ian Malcolm spoke before the American Red Cross in Washington. Sir Eric Drummond broke the proverbial silence of the British civil service by speaking very frankly, before the University Club, of the diplomacy leading up to the war.

EDITORIAL PRAISE

Practically every newspaper in the United States·published glowing tributes to Mr. Balfour. The editors were generous in their praise of him, and convinced that he was the right man in the right place.

In its issue of April twenty-third the New York *Times* printed a long leader, in the course of which it said:

In all the history of the United States there is no precedent for Mr. Balfour's visit, nothing to which it can be compared, nothing that resembles it even remotely. Of all the long list of distinguished Europeans who have come to this country there is not one whose visit has any likeness to his. Most of them came as sightseers.

To Mr. Balfour's expression of "deep gratification" for the privilege and the opportunity of "being connected in any capacity whatever with events which associate Great Britain and the United States in a common effort for a great ideal" the American people respond with the expression of a sentiment not less profound, the satisfaction they have that in taking up arms in a war for freedom, justice, and humanity they place themselves beside the great people of their own blood and speech with whom they share those traditions and principles of democracy which are now battling against absolutism in its last stronghold. A more heartfelt welcome we have never given to visitors from another land than that we now give to the gentlemen of this commission and the distinguished British statesman who is its chief. From the very beginning of the war, throughout this great crisis of civilisation, as Mr. Beck has said, our hearts and minds have disdained to be neutral. We have thrown off the hampering restraints of neutrality and upon that first page in the new chapter of the history of mankind of which Mr. Balfour speaks we are resolved to write a record of American service worthy of this Nation, worthy of the cause we serve and of the obligation we have assumed to our heroic allies.

The members of the British Commission come here upon no mission of ceremony. With them and with the French Commissioners soon to arrive our Government has serious business of consultation and preparation for the part we are to take in beating down the

enemy's resistance. Our pledge of service in the work
of making democracy secure is unconditioned. With
all our resources we commit ourselves to the endeav-
our. From Mr. Balfour, Secretary of State for Foreign Affairs, from the men of high authority in
military and naval affairs and in finance who accompany him, and from the French Commissioners of
like distinction and authority we shall learn how we
can best serve the common cause. They come, as was
plainly intimated in their behalf last night, not to advise or suggest, but to give information that we may
profit by their experience. We are making ready with
such speed as can be commanded by a nation that only
at long intervals hears the call of war. In consultation with our allies, and benefiting by their knowledge,
we shall be able to determine in what ways our strength
can most effectively be put forth.

The conferences at Washington, other conferences
in capitals of our allies to which American Commissioners will be sent, the union of forces for a common
end to be gained by cost and toil and sacrifice common
to all will bind us to our allies in relations of friend-
ship, esteem, and interest that will be of inestimable
value for good understanding, for human progress,
for peace, for the future welfare of mankind. In our
detachment from the war we have felt that we were
in some danger of being left outside the circle of mutual friendships that will bring together the great nations that have fought the fight against the common
peril, a menace to us as to them. That fear we can
now dismiss. We are one with Great Britain, with
France, with Russia, Italy, Belgium, with the other
Old World nations and with those sister republics of
the New World who have made declaration of service

for the "great ideal" of a world made safe for democracy.

ATTENDING CONGRESS

On May fifth Mr. Balfour was invited to attend Congress. This was an astonishing event; for it was the only time in the history of the United States that a British official had been asked to address the House of Representatives. Mr. Malcolm and Mr. Spender-Clay, both members of the House of Commons, were accommodated with special seats on the floor of the House, as a delicate compliment to the House of Commons. Earlier in the week Marshal Joffre and M. Viviani had been welcomed in the Capitol, but the cheers that greeted Mr. Balfour were even greater.

President Wilson, on this momentous occasion, had slipped into the Executive Gallery. No one saw him for a long time. When, finally, he was recognised, the entire House rose, and for several minutes there was a scene, the like of which has not been witnessed in years. An ovation came again when Speaker Clark introduced Mr. Balfour, who seemed deeply affected by the thrilling reception he received. President Wilson joined in the applause and cheering; and when the speaker had concluded and stood below the rostrum with General Bridges, Admiral de Chair, and the British Ambassador, the President

quietly found his way down-stairs and walked
down the line with the Congressmen.

Mr. Balfour made the following address before the House of Representatives:

Will you permit me, on behalf of my friends and
myself, to offer you my deepest and sincerest thanks
for the rare and valued honour which you have done
us by receiving us here to-day? We all feel the greatness of this honour, but I think to none of us can it
come home so closely as to one who, like myself, has
been for forty-three years in the service of a free assembly like your own.

I rejoice to think that a member, a very old member, I am sorry to say, of the British House of Commons, has been received here to-day by this great sister
assembly with such kindness as you have shown to me
and to my friends.

Ladies and gentlemen, these two assemblies are
the greatest and the oldest of the free assemblies now
governing great nations in the world. The history, indeed, of the two is very different. The beginnings of
the British House of Commons go back to a dim historic past, and its full rights and status have only been
conquered and permanently secured after centuries of
political struggle.

Your fate has been a happier one. You were
called into existence at a much later stage of social
development. You came into being complete and per-
fected and all your powers determined and your place
in the constitution secured beyond chance of revolu-
tion, but though the history of these two great assemblies is different, each of them represents the great
democratic principle to which we look forward as the

oeourity for the future peace of the world. All of the free assemblies now to be found governing the great nations of the earth have been modelled either upon your practice or upon ours, or upon both combined.

Mr. Speaker, the compliment paid to the mission from Great Britain by such an assembly and upon such an occasion is one not one of us is ever likely to forget; but there is something, after all, even deeper and more significant in the circumstances under which I now have the honour to address you than any which arise out of the interchange of courtesies, however sincere, between two great and friendly nations.

We all, I think, feel instinctively that this is one of the great moments in the history of the world, and that what is now happening on both sides of the Atlantic represents the drawing together of great and free peoples for mutual protection against the aggression of military despotism.

I am not one of those, none of you are among those, who are such bad democrats as to say that democracies make no mistakes. All free assemblies have made blunders, sometimes they have committed crimes. Why is it then that we look forward to the spirit of free institutions, and especially among our present enemies, as one of the greatest guarantees of the future peace of the world? I will say to you, gentlemen, how it seems to me.

It is quite true that the people and the representatives of the people may be betrayed by some momentary gust of passion into a policy which they ultimately deplore, but it is only a military despotism of the German type that can, through generations, if need be, pursue steadily, remorselessly, unscrupulously, and appallingly the object of dominating the civilisation of mankind. And, mark you, this evil, this menace, under which we are now suffering, is not one which diminishes with the growth of knowledge and progress of material civilisation, but, on the contrary, it increases with them.

When I was young we used to flatter ourselves that progress inevitably meant peace, and that growth of knowledge was always accompanied as its natural fruit by the growth of good-will among the nations of the earth. Unhappily, we know better now, and we know there is such a thing in the world as a power which can with unvarying persistency focus all the resources of knowledge and of civilisation into the one great task of making itself the moral and material master of the world. It is against that danger that we, the free peoples of Western civilisation, have banded ourselves together."

THE NEW YORK WELCOME

In New York, where the members of the British Commission, headed by Mr. Balfour, arrived on May eleventh, the home of Mr. and Mrs. Vincent Astor was placed at their disposal. The party came over from Hoboken, amid hooting craft, to Battery Place. Whistles blew, bells rang, flags were waved, and at every skyscraper window faces appeared, looking out on the river to welcome the distinguished guests to the metropolis. When they landed, Mayor Mitchel and a delegation of prominent citizens greeted the party first at the City Hall. A more splendid reception no visitor to our shores ever received. Over two thousand schoolgirls, dressed in white middy blouses and dark blue skirts, with red hair-ribbons, each carrying a flag, were lined up on the lawn before the City Hall; and behind these, a column of Boy Scouts, in picturesque khaki, in mass and pyramid formations, stood ready to salute.

In a crowded room, in the presence of New York officials, aldermen, and distinguished citizens, Mayor Mitchel formally received the mission. With him was our former Ambassador to Great Britain, Joseph H. Choate, who has since died. Mr. Choate made a brief address of welcome, and then he said, with deep feeling in his voice:

We hesitated, we doubted, we hung back, not from any lack of sympathy, not from any lack of enthusiasm, not because we did not know what was the right path; but how to take it and when to take it was always the question. I feared at one time that we might enter into it for some selfish purpose, for the punishment of aggressions against our individual, national, personal rights, for the destruction of American ships or of a few American lives—ample ground for war; but we waited, and it turns out now that we waited wisely, because we were able at last to enter into this great contest of the whole world for a noble and lofty purpose, such as never attracted nations before. We are entering into it under your lead, sir, for the purpose of the vindication of human rights, for the vindication of free government throughout the world, for the establishment—by and by; soon, we hope; late, it may be—of a peace which shall endure and not a peace that shall be no peace at all.

Fortunately, we have now no room for choice. Under the guidance of the President, we stand pledged now before all the world to all the allies whom we have joined to carry into this contest all that we have, all that we hope for, and all that we ever aspire unto. We shall be in time to take part in that peace which shall forever stand and prevent any more such national outrages as commenced this war on the side of Germany. We have been only thirty days in the war, and already it has had a marvellous effect upon our own people. Before that there was apathy, there was indifference, there was indulgence in personal pursuits, in personal prosperity; but to-day every young man in America and every old man, too, is asking: "What can I do best to serve my country?"

Mr. Balfour then spoke as follows:

Those who had the good fortune to drive through the streets of the city up to this hall, I am sure must have been astounded at the whole-hearted exhibition of enthusiasm which, from every street, from every window, from every house, made itself visible and audible to the spectators. Seldom have I seen a sight —and my experience, alas, is an old one—seldom, or never, have I seen a sight so deeply moving; never have I seen a sight which went more to the heart. If, on the other side of the Atlantic, where the stress and strain of battle seem sometimes hard to sustain, they could have one glimpse of the sympathies shown them

in this vast and noble community, it would give them.
if there be faint hearts—I have not heard of them on
the other side—if faint hearts there be, they indeed
would regain new strength, new courage, new enthusiasm, new resolution, and they would feel again, if
they ever ceased to feel it, that firm determination to
carry through at all sacrifices this great struggle to its
appointed end, which, after all, is the very strength
and nerve of the allied forces.

Never in all her history did New York turn out
so spontaneously to welcome a distinguished man.
The streets were packed at all hours; and people
waited interminably on the chance of catching a
glimpse of Mr. Balfour and his party. Long
before the traffic policemen on bicycles and mo-
torcycles cleared the way, the cheers and cran-
ing of necks began. The American metropolis
frankly laid its work aside and abandoned itself
to a long holiday. Like a beautiful woman, it
draped itself in all its finery; and it borrowed the
bright colours of its allied friends and wove them
into wonderful designs along the avenues everywhere. There wasn't a shop or a home that
didn't put out its flag, and most of them were not
content unless they displayed the union jack too.
Fifth Avenue never looked lovelier. From the
Battery to the Bronx the streets were aflame with
bunting, alive with bands. New York knows how
to entertain; and she was certainly in the right
mood during those momentous days.

THE BANQUET AT THE WALDORF-ASTORIA

In front of the Waldorf-Astoria Hotel there was a particularly splendid display of the allied banners; for a great banquet was to take place here on the evening of May twelfth in honour of both the French and British Commissions. Over a thousand of the city's leading citizens were present. The only two living ex-Presidents came, Taft and Roosevelt; likewise the Governor of the State of New York. The Mayor's Reception Committee had arranged the dinner, and it was probably the most wonderful banquet ever given in America.

The order in which the guests were seated at the high speakers' table was as follows, reading from left to right:

William Fellowes Morgan, President of the Merchants' Association.

W. T. Layton of the Ministry of Munitions.

E. H. Outerbridge, President of the Chamber of Commerce, State of New York.

Sir Eric Drummond.

Dudley Field Malone, Collector of the Port of New York.

The Marquis de Chambrun member of the Chamber of Deputies.

Rear Admiral Nathaniel R. Usher, U. S. Navy.

Rear Admiral Sir Dudley R. S. de Chair, K. C. B., M. V. O.

Frank L. Polk, Counsellor of the State Department.

Vice Admiral Chocheprat, Senior Vice Admiral of the French Navy.

Joseph H. Choate, Chairman, Mayor's Citizens' Committee.

Sir Cecil Spring-Rice, British Ambassador.

Theodore Roosevelt.

Marshal Joffre.

Charles S. Whitman, Governor of the State of New York.

The Right Hon. Arthur James Balfour.

J. P. Mitchel, Mayor of New York.

René Viviani.

William M. Calder, United States Senator.

Jules J. Jusserand, the French Ambassador.

William H. Taft.

Sir Thomas White, Minister of Finance of Canada.

Dr. Nicholas Murray Butler.

Gen. G. T. M. Bridges, C. M. G., D. S. O.

Major Gen. Leonard Wood, U. S. A.

The Right Hon. Lord Cunliffe.

W. A. Prendergast.

Sir S. H. Lever.

General Harry F. Hodges.

M. Hovalacque.

Horace Porter.

Ian Malcolm, M. P.

Hugh Gibson.

Joseph H. Choate again delivered the principal speech on behalf of the city. He followed Mayor Mitchel, and said, in part:

America, from the Atlantic to the Pacific, from the Lakes to the Gulf, America has learned what this war

is about, what it is for—that it is for the establishment
of freedom against slavery, for the vindication of free
government against tyranny, and oppression, and autocracy, and all the other horrible names that you can
apply to misgovernment.   When it came to that, there
was but one question for America, and our President
at Washington has solved it for us.   Nobody can tell
how far he saw ahead any more than we at this moment can tell how far we can see ahead.

THE MEANING OF THE WAR

Mr. Balfour spoke of the meaning of the war,
and his speech follows:

I have not come here authorised by my Government to set myself up or to set my friends up as in-
structors of the great American people.   They know
and you know how to manage your affairs, and do not
require us to teach you.   It may be, it probably is, the
fact, that a study of the history of this war will show
those who run and desire to read that there are certain mistakes which a great democracy, imperfectly
prepared for war, may easily make.   We shall be
happy to describe these mistakes to you, if happily it
will be your desire to learn the lesson from them.   But
I do not propose either now or at any other occasion
to set myself up as an adviser or monitor on these
great themes.   It is enough that I proclaim my unalterable conviction that we have reached a moment in
the world's history on which the future, not of this
country, but of every country, not of its interests, but
of every interest of civilisation is trembling in the bal-
ance.   At that critical moment it is my bounden duty

to raise my voice and to appeal to all who will listen
to me to-day in the great task which we have been
bearing for two and a half years, and which you
have cheerfully and generously determined to take the
weight of upon your own shoulders. . . .

Why is it that the people of this great city have
come forth instinctively—I was going to say by thousands; I feel inclined to say by millions—to show their
enthusiasm for the cause you have taken up? It is because they instinctively feel what is the vital issue at
stake, because they instinctively feel that it is neither
desirable nor, were it desirable, possible for this great
Republic to hold itself aloof from a world in suffering
and not do its part to redeem mankind.

Surely it is a significant fact that here we are, the
representatives of three great democracies, in the very
heart of New York, to plead a common cause. What
has brought us all together? What is the meaning of
this unique gathering? What is the meaning of the
multitude crowding your streets to-day and yesterday?
It is a shallow view to suppose that each of these great
nations has had a separate and different cause of controversy with the enemy—that Russia was dragged
in because of Serbia, that France was dragged in because of Russia, that Great Britain was dragged in because of the violation of Belgian territory, and that the
United States has been dragged in because of the
piratical warfare of the German submarines.

All those causes are, each of them, and separately,
no doubt a sufficient reason, but for a moment to con-
sider this war carried on by the Allies as that of separate interests, separate causes of controversy, is an
utterly inadequate and false view of the situation.
These are but symptoms of the absolute necessity in

LIEUT.-GENERAL G. T. M. BRIDGES, C.M.G., D.S.O., AND REAR-ADMIRAL
SIR DUDLEY DE CHAIR, R.N., K.C.B., M.V.O., OFFICER OF THE
LEGION OF HONOR.
The Chief Naval and Military members of the Mission.

which a civilised world finds itself, to deal with an im-
minent and overmastering peril. What is that peril?
What is it we feel that we have got to stop? I will
tell you my view of it. It is the calculated and re-
morseless use of every civilised weapon to carry out
the ends of pure barbarism. To us of English speech
it seems impossible, incredible, that a nation should
clearly set itself to work and co-ordinate every means
of science, every means that knowledge, that industry
can provide, not for the bettering of its own people,
but for the demolition of other peoples.

The history of the world is too full of the ad-
ventures of unscrupulous ambition. We know, all
through history, of men who have endeavoured, at the
cost of others, to expand their own State. Within
the last century, or a little more, we have seen men of
genius trying to coerce the world. But this is not a
case of a new Napoleon arising to carry out a new adventure. This is not a case of adventure, of a genius
seeking to satisfy his ambition within the limits of
his own country.

It is something far different and far more dangerous for mankind. It is the settled determination to
use every means to put the whole world at her feet.
We all know it is a commonplace that science has enor-
mously expanded the means by which men can kill
each other. Modern destruction is carried out as
much in the laboratory of your universities as it is
on the field of battle, but we have always believed,
we have always hoped, that this increased power of
destruction would be limited and controlled by the
growing forces of humanity and civilisation. We
have been taught, not by Germany, but by those who
rule Germany, by the military caste which controls

Germany—we have been taught a different lesson, and
we now know not merely that every scientific weapon
will be put in force to make war more horrible than it
was in barbarous times, but that even the rights of
civilisation, of trade, of commerce, even the intercom-
munication between different peoples, will be used for
the same sinister object.

Ladies and gentlemen that is the danger we have
to meet, and if at this moment the world is bathed
in blood and tears from the highlands of distant Ar-
menia down to the very fields of France, almost within
sight of the Straits of Dover—if we have seen a reck-
less destruction of life, not merely of soldiers but
of civilians; if we have seen peaceful communities
dragged through the mire, ruined, outraged; if horror
has been heaped upon horror, until really we almost
get callous in reading our newspapers in the morning
—if all these things are true, shall we not rise up and
resist them?

Shall we who know what freedom is become the
humble and obsequious servants of those who only
know what power is? That will never be tolerated.
The free nations of the earth are not thus to be crushed
out of existence, and if any proof is required that that
consummation is impossible, it is a gathering like this
where the three great democracies of the West are
joined together under circumstances unique in the
whole history of the world.

And that fact should also give strength and conso-
lation to those who, feeling the magnitude of the issue
at stake, are inclined to doubt how the contest will end.
But we will fail unless all here who love liberty are
prepared to labour together, to fight together, to make
our sacrifices in common—unless that happens we may

be destroyed piecemeal and the civilisation of the world may receive a wound from which it will not easily recover.

M. Viviani, of course, also spoke, in French. He said that the Kultur of Germany was all very well until its interests were crossed, and then it became like a wild beast. Germany did not know the spirit of England, of France, of Russia. "You in America," he went on, in his impassioned way, "cannot realise, cannot imagine the suffering and horror of what war has meant to France and her people. But you will arouse yourselves to the battle for liberty, justice, democracy, and humanity. . . . I see before me now the might and strength of Germany and realise that it must —that it will—be overthrown."

After this great banquet, Mr. Balfour went to the home of Mr. and Mrs. Cornelius Vanderbilt. There Dr. Nicholas Murray Butler, President of Columbia University, presented him with the diploma of Doctor of Laws. Mr. Balfour seemed greatly moved; and in his speech in reply he said that he had never been so touched in all his life as at the thrilling reception New York had given him and his party.

THE CHAMBER OF COMMERCE LUNCHEON

The New York Chamber of Commerce tendered a luncheon to Mr. Balfour, at which more than a thousand people were present. Mr. E. H. Outerbridge, the President, presided, and Mr. Balfour was again given a fine ovation when he rose to express his thanks and to say that the dream of his whole life had been to see "the union between the English-speaking, freedom-loving branches of the human race drawn far closer than in the past, the time when all temporary causes of difference which may ever have separated the two great peoples would be seen in their true and just proportion; and," he went on, "I hope we shall all realise, on whatever side of the Atlantic fortune has placed us, that the things wherein we have differed in the past sink into absolute insignificance when compared with those vital agreements which at all times, but never more than at such a time as the present, unite us in one great spiritual whole."

In alluding to the bonds between the English-speaking races, he said:

You have absorbed in your midst many admirable citizens drawn from all parts of Europe, whom American institutions and American ways of thought have moulded and are moulding into one great people. I rejoice to think it should be so. A similar process on a small scale is going on in the self-governing dominions of the British Empire. It is a good process, it is a noble process. Let us never forget that wherever be the place in which that great and beneficent process is going on, whether it be in Canada, whether it be in

Australia, or whether on the largest scale of all it be in the United States of America, the spirit which the immigrant absorbs is the spirit in all these places largely due to a historic past in which your forefathers and my forefathers, gentlemen, all had their share.

In speaking of the Chairman's reference to the splendid work of the British fleet, Mr. Balfour said:

Does anybody think that if the sea power were transferred from British to German hands the historian of the future could say the same of the German fleet? By their fruits we know them. Deliberately brought into existence in the hope that it would break down that naval power which the German autocracy— not the German people, but the German autocracy— recognises as one of the greatest bulwarks of freedom, and one of the most powerful defences against world domination, knowing that instinctively, they have been feverishly building for eighteen or twenty years in order that, if it might be so, they could destroy the country with which they had no quarrel, and no cause of quarrel, but which they regarded with an instinctive and unalterable jealousy. They have been disappointed. Their fleet remains safely in the harbour.

What puts out to sea is not the battleship or the battle cruiser; there is no successor of the great fleets of ancient times; but the submarine which, in their hands, finds its natural prey in the destruction of defenceless merchantmen and the butchery of defenceless women and children. I will do the German fleet the justice to say that I do not believe that this was its ideal when this war started, or when its ships were

under construction. What I do say is that the use
which the German governing classes are now making
of this new weapon, while it will never decide the issue
of this war, nevertheless indicates a menace to the
future commerce of the world which must be absolutely stopped for the future. Under the old maritime laws, which the United States and Great Britain
in particular have always recognised, fleets undoubtedly did interfere with the commerce of any enemy
belligerents, and it is very difficult to see how that
could or ought to be avoided until that happy time
comes when war is neither on land nor sea permitted
to interfere with private rights, or indeed permitted to
go on at all.

But, gentlemen, maritime warfare as it has been
carried on by civilised nations in the past has been a
human affair, carried out under recognised laws, under which as little injury was done to the neutral trader
as was possible under the circumstances, compared to
the abominations which are now insisted upon by the
German staff. Huge tracts of ocean are marked out
at the arbitrary will of one belligerent, and within
these vast areas neutrals, peaceable traders, do not
merely have their ships taken in, adjudged in the prize
court, dealt with, and non-belligerent life carefully regarded, but they are sunk at sea, no examination, no
knowledge of what is in the ship, no knowledge of the
character of the crew, no knowledge of whether there
are or are not passengers aboard, no knowledge of the
goods which are being transported, of the place from
which they came or the destination designed. That,
gentlemen, is carrying out the methods of barbarism,
and in a manner which would have been regarded as
incredible even in Germany two years ago. It has

been carried out by a Government which, when it thought worth while for diplomatic reasons, was never wearied of talking of the freedom of the seas.

But it is a method of conducting warfare which in its indirect consequences, as well as its direct consequences, is of such a character that the civilised world must, when this war is over, take effectual precautions against its repetition. For, if not, it seems to me that, whenever two countries go to war, and whenever it suits the least scrupulous of the belligerents, not merely will a great wrong have been inflicted upon its opponent, but the commerce of the whole civilised world will be disorganised and destroyed. That is impossible to tolerate. And this Chamber has under its guardianship the interests of trade and commerce, and it is of all bodies the one most interested in seeing that, so long as wars are still permitted—and I hope that will not be long—maritime warfare shall be conducted under methods consistent with public law, consistent with ordinary humanity, consistent with those fundamental principles of morality which underlie—or ought to underlie—all law.

When this tremendous conflict has drawn to its appointed close, and when, as I believe, victory shall have crowned our joint efforts, there will arise not merely between nations but within nations a series of problems which will tax all our statesmanship to deal with. I look forward to that time, not, indeed, wholly without anxiety, but in the main with hope and with confidence; and one of the reasons for that hope and one of the foundations of that confidence is to be found in the fact that your nation and my nation will have so much to do with the settlement of the questions.

I do not think anybody will accuse me of being insensible to the genius and to the accomplishments of other nations. I am one of those who believe that only in the multitude of different forms of culture can the completed movement of progress have all the variety in unity of which it is capable; and, while I admire other cultures, and while I recognise how absolutely all-important they are to the future of mankind, I do think that among the English-speaking peoples is especially and peculiarly to be found a certain political moderation in all classes which gives one the surest hope of dealing in a reasonable, progressive spirit with social and political difficulties. And without that reasonable moderation interchanges are violent, and as they are violent, reactions are violent also, and the smooth advance of humanity is seriously interfered with.

I believe that on this side of the Atlantic, and I hope on the other side of the Atlantic, if and when these great problems have actively to be dealt with, it will not be beyond the reach of your statesmanship, or of our own, to deal with them in such a manner that we cannot merely look back upon this great war as the beginning of a time of improved international relations, of settled peace, of deliberate refusal to pour out oceans of blood to satisfy some notion of domination; but that in addition to those blessings the war, and what happens after the war, may prove to be the beginning of a revivified civilisation, which will be felt in all departments of human activity, which will not merely touch the material but also the spiritual side of mankind, and which will make the second decade of the twentieth century memorable in the history of mankind.

A MESSAGE TO THE STEEL WORKERS

Through Representative John G. Cooper, Mr. Balfour sent, on May seventh, a message to the steel workers of the Mahoning Valley. It read:

I hope you will on my behalf give a very warm greeting to the steel workers of the Mahoning Valley. I know well that they have fully realised the vital importance of this war to the security and honour of their country and to the cause of freedom throughout the world. I hope that they will also realise how much they can do in their individual capacity for the common cause of promoting the output of material on which a plentiful supply so much depends.

It is only through strenuous exertion and zealous co-operation of the allied belligerent powers that victory is possible. With these assured, then victory is not merely possible, but assured.

BALFOUR VISITS ROOSEVELT

It was on Sunday afternoon, May thirteenth, that Mr. Balfour made his mysterious visit to Sagamore Hill to see his old acquaintance, Theodore Roosevelt. These two great men had met in 1910, after the Colonel's return from his famous African hunt, and again in 1914, when Roosevelt stopped in England after returning from Madrid, where he had attended the wedding of his son Kermit.

What they said to each other on this particular

day no one knows; but Mr. Balfour remained
with the Colonel for four hours. Neither gave
out an interview after the visit, and even the
most diligent press correspondents failed to get
an inkling of what took place. Some of the
papers had it that Colonel Roosevelt's proposed
division for France was mentioned. Perhaps it
was. At any rate, Mr. Balfour did not leave
Sagamore Hill until about ten o'clock—he had
remained for "high tea"—and the Colonel waved
good-bye to him from the veranda. There had
been no other guests, save Mr. Balfour's parliamentary secretary, Ian Malcolm, and Colonel
Roosevelt's son, Quentin.

HONOURED BY THE PHI BETA KAPPA SOCIETY

On May seventeenth Mr. Balfour was hon-
oured by the Phi Beta Kappa Society, through an
initiation conducted by Lyon G. Typer, President
of the College of William and Mary, Virginia.
The brief ceremony took place at the Long residence, in Washington, which was occupied by the
British Commission. In his speech of acceptance,
Mr. Balfour said:

Mr. President and Brethren of the Phi Beta Kappa
Society: I, on behalf of myself and on behalf of my
friends, thank you for allowing us to take part in
this service, the memory of which will rest with us
as long as life exists. You have welcomed us as the

mission from Great Britain. You have welcomed those members of the mission who belonged to sister universities on the other side of the Atlantic, and you have conferred upon us the highest honour which you can give or which is in our power to receive. We most sincerely thank you for what you have done.

In the eloquent and moving speeches which have to-day been delivered by your President and others who have taken part in the ceremonies, little has been said of matters strictly academic. They were present to our minds, but they lay, and rightly lay, in the background. You who are present represent, and, in a lesser degree, I suppose we can claim to represent, the academic life and training of the two great countries, and the fact that we should meet together and deal in the main with matters which are international and political, rather than with matters which are in the strictest and narrowest sense academic, shows the great truth, or what I deem to be a great truth, that learning and study, if they be divorced from the realities of life and social life, lose more than half their worth.

I understand, and others this morning have reminded us, that this meeting is a symbol of all that represents the culture and education, or most of what represents the culture and education, in these two great nations that are now united in the pursuit of one great common cause. Let us take it for granted, then.

The history of the society, of which we are the youngest members, is a happy illustration of the truth which I have just insisted upon; for, if I rightly understand the history of the society, it was born in the stress and conflict of a great national crisis. The crisis we are living through to-day is possibly a greater

crisis than that which struck this country in 1776 It
is one the importance of which extends far beyond
the boundaries of this community and touches the
whole world, not in America alone, not in Europe
only, but wherever the ideals of Christian civilisation
have come to flourish.

Gentlemen, it surely is a great thing to feel that
all of us who have in common a university training,
whether it has been carried out here or in Britain,
have the same noble traditions which have been main-
tained for all these centuries; it is a great thing to feel
that we are one.   You, Mr. President, observed, with
truth, that we are largely if not wholly of a common
stock, but that blood is but a poor cement—I think
that was your phrase—is but a poor and weak cement,
if that which it is meant to cement is not bound together by ties, spiritual ties, more fervent and more
gripping than anything that could be conferred by any
accident of heredity.   That surely is so.

Whether they are students of American universities or whether they are students of British universities, they have a bond of union stronger than language,
than literature, than law.   Stronger these bonds are
and should be.   They have the bond of common hopes,
of common purposes, of nations making common sacrifices for one great end, and that end is not only that
of American universities and British universities, not
merely the future culture or economic progress of these
two great and free communities, but in addition to
these causes, in themselves sufficiently great to fill the
minds and kindle the imaginations of even the most
sluggish, we can surely say for ourselves that we have
in our guardianship, gathered here to-day, that we
have in our keeping, the future freedom of the world,

and that success in our efforts means the future civilisation of the world.

These are thoughts which I should hardly have ventured to refer to on such an occasion as this, before a society so strictly academic in its character as this, had not the example been set in the noble address of your President and others, and I should otherwise not have trespassed beyond the relatively narrow bounds of purely academic interests and ventured to go into those wider spheres of policy and humanity which are in all our thoughts at this great and solemn moment of our history.

On behalf of my friends and myself I beg to thank you for the greatest honour which you could possibly confer or which we could possibly receive.

After this speech, Mr. Balfour called on the President to say good-bye.

RICHMOND

Richmond, the capital of the Confederacy, rich in the traditions of the old English cavalier days, welcomed the mission on May nineteenth, in the name of the whole South, with a warmth and spontaneity unequalled during the mission's stay in this country. Received with a salute of nineteen guns, entertained at the historic executive mansion amidst the portraits of many Royal governors, and acclaimed to the echo at a crowded mass-meeting at the auditorium, Mr. Balfour and his fellow officials probably felt more at home in the old Confederate capital than at any other place they stopped.

The mission was particularly desirous, on its official call upon the South, to pay homage to the gallant Southern leaders who fought so bravely a half century ago.   Lieut.-General Bridges placed wreaths in the name of the British army on the tombs of Robert E. Lee, Stonewall Jackson, and General J. E. B. Stuart and made the earnest prediction that the lessons of leadership, courage, and endurance taught by those men would not find their succesors unworthy of their memories to-day.

Mr. Balfour, after a triumphal procession through the flag-decked streets to the auditorium, was greeted by a large Southern audience which showed how truly its two great struggles of the past had been forgotten by singing both "God Save the King" and "The Star Spangled Banner."   After expressing his joy at the decision to send American troops to Europe, Mr. Balfour said:

Out of the manhood of America there will flow, I am sure, the best fighting material in the world, and the only limit to that flow will be the limit imposed by the material difficulties of transport and equipment. The United States has greater resources for modern warfare than any other nation in the world.   I do not refer to numbers alone; I refer rather to that courage, resolution, inventiveness, which alone make numbers efficient. Though unprepared, as we were unprepared, you are filled with that spirit which will bring results as encouraging to your friends as they will be discouraging to your foes.

Germany cannot succeed in this war. Success does not lie along the paths of frightfulness and ruthlessness. That nation which has known no law, either of charity or of love, which has cast all scruples to the wind, which has allowed no consideration to stand in its way, that nation has raised up outraged civilisation to make certain its own defeat.

Mr. Balfour regretted deeply that time did not permit a longer tour through the South. And if Richmond's reception could be any augury, that feeling would indeed be well-founded, for the city was given over body and soul to its distinguished visitors.

One of the most amusing incidents of Mr. Balfour's whole visit occurred on the way home. By special request of a few leading townspeople, the train stopped for a few minutes at Fredericksburg for a scene which would have dumbfounded Mr. Balfour's more old-fashioned friends. Great Britain's Foreign Secretary, tall, earnest, with a finely intellectual face, came out onto the rear platform of the train to greet a motley group of swarthy, dirt-grimed railroad men, coloured ragamuffins, mystified hangers-on, and a small official reception committee in formal dress, who handed up to him a bouquet of roses.

Mr. Balfour, strangely enough, made one of the warmest speeches of his whole trip. Meanwhile, Bill Nye, the ubiquitous Secret Service man, familiar with rear-end speeches through his trips with the Presidents, stood watch in hand beside him to time three minutes. Time up, Bill reached out his hand to twitch the speaker's coat-tail, remembered it was not a President but a British Foreign Secretary who was speaking, and lost his nerve. Four minutes passed, five; the engineer tooted, the conductor shouted "All aboard," Bill's fingers got more and more nervous, and still felicitous phrases flowed from Mr. Balfour's lips. Finally, after seven minutes, the train got under way.

Mr. Balfour laughed about it afterwards and referred to it himself as his "electioneering tour."

CHICAGO REGRETFULLY OMITTED

It had been planned, of course, that the British Mission should pay a visit to Chicago; but it was found that there was too much to be done in Washington and New York to make the trip possible. It must be remembered that the British Mission was a working mission. Meetings were held, even at breakfast, between the United States officials and the members of the British Mission. Not a moment was lost. Afterwards, from the border, Mr. Balfour sent a warm message to Mayor Thompson and the city of Chicago, regretting that he could not find time to visit the metropolis of the Middle West.

THE PRESIDENT CALLS ON BALFOUR

On May twenty-first President Wilson called upon Mr. Balfour at the British Mission, and spent almost an hour with him. There was, however, no report given out as to what they discussed. The shipping situation, which was conceded to be one of vast importance, was talked over by Mr. Balfour twice that same afternoon,— once with his own trade experts and later with Chairman Denman and General Goethals then of the Shipping Board.

THE SPEECH BEFORE THE COTTON MANUFAC-TURERS

American cotton manufacturers met in Washington on May twenty-second, to appoint a War Committee for co-operation with the Government, and they were addressed by Mr. Balfour, who was introduced by Secretary of the Navy Daniels. His reception was most enthusiastic. In return, he said:

None of us suspected when this great war was started that the United States, thousands of miles away, would be drawn into it.' And yet I think in looking back that the logic of events was irresistible.

From the beginning there has been but one choice, and that choice inevitable. The United States has not hesitated to take it, and now that she has taken it she will not withdraw, I am confident, until the objects sought are attained.

Germany, by her insensate policies, has forced this country of unbounded resources to throw all her power, all her wealth, but, more than that, all her moral strength, into the issue. America seeks no vulgar ends, no territorial aggrandisement, no mean gain. All of us would feel defeated and dishonoured if we did not leave the world free from the menace that is hanging over it, that has been growing every decade, yes, every month, more dangerous.

Only the historian of the far future will be able to see all the causes and all the cross currents of this monster struggle. We here to-day cannot project our gaze sufficiently to envisage it all. The world's history has been full of the outpourings of blood, the squandering of money and the wastage of resources in war, and in almost every case the impartial historian has been able to find something to say for both sides. I do honestly feel, however, that there will be no hesitation or doubt possible in this present war.

As the war began with the cynical, outrageous oppression of a little nation away down in the Balkans and went through the brutal violation of another small country to the north, so it is continuing. No excuse can be offered for the cold-blooded, calculating aggression which has marked the course of the military autocracy, which has plunged not only Europe but every quarter of the civilised globe into untold suffering and raised up for itself an undreamed-of vengeance.

THE HON. SIR ERIC DRUMMOND, K.C.M.G., C.B.
Private Secretary to Mr. Balfour.
Formerly Private Secretary to Lord Grey and Mr. Asquith.

THE NATIONAL PRESS CLUB SPEECH

Before the National Press Club, on the afternoon of May twenty-fourth, in a farewell address in recognition of the gratitude expressed by the correspondents for his consideration of the press, Mr. Balfour spoke as follows:

Mr. President and Gentlemen of the Press Club: You, sir, in your opening remarks, reminded me of the first day of my visit in this city and have quoted one or two things that I then appear to have said to the representatives of the press. That was about a month ago, and certainly, so far as I am concerned, the month that has elapsed since that fateful day has been filled with impressions the most pleasurable, the most momentous; impressions which will never fade from my memory while memory lasts; impressions of which I hope to give some faint and imperfect account, it may be, but still some account, to those I have left on the other side of the Atlantic and who are engaged in the same great struggle and the same world work to which all of you are contributing so important a share.

Gentlemen, I came to the United States conscious, of course, of the importance of the mission with which I have been intrusted by my Government; conscious, as your President has said this afternoon, that the mission, from the very nature of the case, was one of the most important in which either of our two countries has ever concerned itself; conscious that the very condition of the world in which we lived gave weight and importance to every action, to every word, and to every report of every word, which might take place during its existence.

Now, gentlemen, nobody knows better than I how much you and the great press that you represent have contributed to whatever measure of success our mission may have obtained.

It is perfectly true that the primary duty intrusted to us was that of discussing with the Government of the United States the numberless matters of importance which have to be decided if two great countries find themselves co-operating in one gigantic task.

The kindness with which we were received, the warmth of the welcome which reached us from all parts of the country, soon made it plain that the strictly and narrowly business side of our mission was not the only one which was important at the present juncture. After all, the co-operation of two great countries is not merely the question of working through the instrumentality of experts, the sending of men here or there, the proper distribution of your naval forces, the method by which the financial co-operation can best be secured, or all the other endless questions which have come up for daily discussion. Those are all important. They do not stand alone. Something more than that, if a mission be fortunate, may come of its work, something which has not got to do with naval, military, or financial details, but which, in the phrase —I think it is of Burke—comes home to the feelings and bosoms of men. There is something in a sympathetic and mutual comprehension; there is something the worth of which cannot indeed be estimated merely by enumerating army corps or millions or billions of dollars, the cataloguing of destroyers, but which is represented by something different, more spiritual, as important: a sympathy of soul between two great and free peoples, who are not only engaged on a common task, but who are conscious of their mutual co-operation.

Now, gentlemen, for my own part, I have felt more deeply than I find it easy to express the kindness of the reception which you have given to the mission in general and to myself in particular. That kindness has been shown me, lavishly shown me, in Washington. It was shown not less fully and not less lavishly in New York and in Richmond, and I only mourn that the inevitable exigencies of public business make it impossible for me to visit other parts of the United States, to communicate directly and personally with men in the Middle West, in the Far West, and in other portions of this colossal territory, which is already occupied by the most powerful community in the world, and which is, I think, destined in the future to have an abiding influence for all that makes for peaceful civilisation and freedom, and which has certainly shown on the present occasion that a great community can be moved to perform great sacrifices for an ideal which has in it nothing of selfishness, nothing of the petty appetite for power, nothing but a pure and unstained desire to benefit the cause of civilisation and of mankind.

Gentlemen, that is the impression which I have received from the living intercourse that I have been able to have with a fraction—I admit, too small a fraction, but not an unimportant fraction—of this great State. It would have been impossible for me to have obtained the impressions I have received, or to have given the impressions I have desired to give, without the assistance of the press of this country.

You, and those with whom you work, have, after all, supplied the sensory nerves which permeate the whole country from end to end and make what happens in Washington or New York, or wherever it may be, the common property of the whole American people. It is a colossal power. It is a power whose magnitude it is very difficult—it is impossible, I think—to over-estimate. It is a power very easily abused. It is a power which those who possess it have to be cautious as to whether in the ordinary work of what, after all, has a business side, and purely a business side, they may not commit some injury to the public weal which they certainly never contemplated when they did it, and for which, perhaps, they might rarely regard themselves as directly responsible.

Gentlemen, you have shown, during the month's experience which I have had of your labours, shown that the American press is animated by the highest patriotic principles, that it is incapable, or has shown itself, so far as I am concerned, as incapable of misrepresenting or perverting in the smallest particular anything which I may have said or done. I know that it is to you and your friends that any word I have spoken, be it worth listening to or not worth listening to, at all events reaches unperverted those for whom it is intended. For that I wish to express to you my most grateful thanks for what you have done since I have been here.

Your President quoted an appeal which I appear to have made—I have forgotten the exact circumstance—to some of your number a month ago. Never was an appeal more generously listened to or more faithfully accepted, both in the spirit and the letter, and I beg most sincerely to thank you for the way in which you have exercised your duties in connection with the mission for which I am responsible. These are, I suppose, the last words that I shall say in public before I leave the hospitable area of your great country. May I not only thank you, as I have just imperfectly tried to do, for the share you have taken in any such success as the mission may have had, but may I, through you, thank that much larger public to whom you appeal for the unprecedented personal kindness which they have shown to me and to all those that accompany me.

I came with high hopes to Washington. Those hopes have been far surpassed by the reality. I expected, from what I knew of American friends on the other side of the Atlantic, that I should be received with kindness, with courtesy, and with sympathy; but the kindness, the courtesy and the sympathy which I have received are far in excess of anything which I dared hope for, or anything which I can pretend even to myself to have deserved. It is a sad thought to me that the moment of parting has come, and that those whom I looked upon as my friends before I knew them, and who have become my friends in very truth and indeed since I knew them, I shall be separated from, at all events, during the continuance of the present war. After that it may be my happy lot to return in a less responsible and official position to renew the connection for a moment severed by the tragic events in which we are all equally concerned.

But, gentlemen, the mission could not stay here forever. It has received a welcome, a welcome which none of its members will forget, and to me falls the pleasant duty on my own behalf and on behalf of my friends, of saying to you and to all whom you can reach how deeply we thank the American public for what they have done, how warm our recollection of their kindness, and, above all and more than all, how we leave this country even more convinced than we came to it, that the United States of America, when they take a great cause in hand, a cause which appeals to none of the lower motives which animate communities as they may animate individuals, which appeals only to what is highest and best in the national conscience, when, I say, the American people take in hand a cause of which that may be said, they are not going to relinquish the pursuit, they are not for a moment going to relax their endeavours to bring the great enterprise to a successful conclusion, until that successful conclusion is indeed safely within our grasp. That is the message which I shall take away from these shores.

There are those who have said that the preparations made by the United States are proceeding slowly and haltingly, and that a country which has been in the war for some forty days ought to have done far more than has actually been accomplished. For my own part, I think those who speak in accents like these know very little of the actual way in which public life is and must be carried on in free countries. At the beginning of the forty days of which I speak no preparations had been made; the country was anxiously, indeed, watching the events; it had not begun to make any of the preparations necessary for taking a part in a gigantic struggle.

I think that what has been performed in those forty days is most remarkable. It is quite true that the action of the Executive Government may be delayed, and has been delayed, by the fact that certain measures placed before Congress took some time to pass; some of them have not yet passed. But I have lived with representative assemblies all my life, and who is it that supposes that representative assemblies are going to make great and new departures in public policy solely at the waving of a wand? Such expectations are vain. It is useless to entertain them, and, for my own part, I am quite confident—I perhaps feel more confident than it seems to me one who has had no personal experience of American politics should feel—but, speaking for myself, I feel quite confident that Congress will not refuse to the President and the Government of the country all powers, great as they are, which are absolutely necessary if the war is to be successfully pursued. I am not only persuaded that it will give those powers, but I am persuaded that when these powers are given they will be used to the utmost with as little delay as the imperfection of human institutions and of human beings allow, to throw the great and, I believe, the decisive weight of America to the full extent into the great contest.

That is my belief. In that belief I shall leave these shores. In that belief I shall make my report to the Allied Governments, so far as I can reach them, on the other side of the Atlantic, and in that belief I look forward with a cheerful confidence to days which will undoubtedly be days of trial and difficulty, but beyond which we can surely see the dawn of a happier day, coming not merely to the kindred communities to which we belong, but to all mankind and all nations which love liberty and pursue righteousness.

Mr. President, I will say no more. I thank you. Through you I thank every well-wisher in America for all that you have done for me and for my friends. I wish you a farewell. I wish for a reunion at no distant date under happier circumstances, when we can meet, not feeling that we have to deal with a great crisis which requires all our capacity, all our courage, and all our perseverance, but that we can look back upon trials already successfully passed, upon days happily accomplished, upon a permanent peace for ourselves and for the rest of the world. Those are my hopes, Mr. President, and none can aid more efficiently than the gentlemen I am addressing in the fulfilment of the ideals which I am quite sure are common to all who speak our language, and to many others who sympathise with our aspirations.

I beg to thank you.

BACK TO CANADA

On May twenty-fifth the Balfour party left United States soil and crossed into Canada. The conferences which had taken place were thought to have been of vast importance in shaping the policy of the war.

Mayor Church, of Toronto, received Mr. Balfour on the afternoon of the same day. A special guard of honour of fifty men from an overseas company of the 109th Battalion was lined up at the station. One of the speakers charged Mr. Balfour not to forget that he was among countrymen now, as well as among friends, whereupon the distinguished statesman immediately replied:

I did not need that invitation to entertain this sentiment. I have left on the other side of the border a nation of friends. I come into Canada, to a great free country, composed not only of friends, but of countrymen. We think the same thoughts, we live in the same civilisation, we belong to the same empire, and if anything could have cemented more closely the bonds of the empire, if anything could have made us feel that we were indeed of one flesh and one blood with one common history behind us, if anything could have cemented these feelings, it is the consciousness that now for two years and a half we have been engaged in this great struggle, in which, I thank God, all North America is now as one.

We have been engaged in this great struggle these two years and a half, fighting together, when necessary making all our sacrifices in common, working together toward a common and victorious end, which no doubt will crown our efforts.

IN OTTAWA

Mr. Balfour reached Ottawa on May twenty-seventh, where the Governor General's Foot Guards met him at the station and escorted him to Rideau Hall. Here they were formally received and welcomed by Sir Robert Borden, the Prime Minister, and many other Government officials. The next day, before the two houses of the Canadian Parliament, Mr. Balfour made a ringing speech, in which he declared that "democracy could not fail." Then he went on:

I know the democracies of the Old World and the New will come out of this struggle, not merely trium-

phant in the military sense, but strengthened in their
own inner life, more firmly convinced that the path of
freedom is the only path to national greatness.

I do not believe that anything more unexpected to
the outside world ever occurred than the enthusiastic
self-sacrifice with which the great self-governing British dominions have thrown themselves into the great
contest at the side of the motherland.

Foreign speculators about the British Empire, before the war began, said to themselves that this loosely
constructed State resembled nothing that ever existed
in history before, that it was held together by no coer-
cive power, that the mother country could not raise a
corporal's guard in Canada, Australia, New Zealand,
or wherever you will; that she could not raise a shil-
ling by taxation.

She had no power except the power which a certain class of politician never remembers—the moral
power of affection, sentiment, common aims, and common ideals. Even those of us who believed the new
experiment of the British Empire was going to succeed felt it was difficult that so vast an empire, so
loosely knit, should be animated by one soul, or that
the indirect thrill of common necessity should go from
end to end.

No greater miracle has ever happened in the history of civilisation than the way in which the co-ordinated British democracies worked together with a
uniform spirit of self-sacrifice in the cause in which
they believed: not merely their own individual security,
but the safety of the empire and the progress of civilisation, and liberty itself, were at stake.

MONTREAL—AND HOME AGAIN

Montreal welcomed Balfour and his Commission on May thirtieth, in fitting fashion. Soon thereafter, in secret, the entire British party sailed for England.

It had been a triumphant tour from beginning to end. Soon the results will tell the story better than mere words.

Back on home soil, the Manchester *Guardian*, perhaps the leading Liberal paper of England, printed this splendid editorial. America approves of such an envoy as is suggested.

MR. BALFOUR'S FAREWELL

Mr. Balfour, bidding farewell to the United States yesterday, remarked that "this mission could not stay forever." We are not sure. At least, if Mr. Balfour's Mission has been as great a success as every one appears to agree that it has been, there would appear to be good reason why we should have either permanently or at frequent intervals in the United States a special envoy of his peculiar distinction and authority. Mr. Balfour has made an impression on American opinion, as we expected he would, alike by the fine tone of his utterances with regard to the cause of the Allies and the reasons which have drawn the United States into the war, and by his tact, courtesy, and accessibility. But he has also done a great deal of good spade-work in accomplishing his main object of making easier cooperation between the United States and the Allies.

Many conferences have been held on all the chief aspects of the conduct of the war, and various experts remain to carry on the task of mutual help. Mr. Balfour returns to fulfil the second part of his duty, for he can now, again with a special degree of authority, give most valuable information to the British Government about the way in which America is organising herself for war, the precise aims which she has before her, and the kind of peace settlement that she has in view. His is thus a double service. We are certain that it has great value, and if so it should be worth repeating, whether by Mr. Balfour or another. We have suffered throughout the war from imperfect communication between the Allies. It is especially important in the case of the United States that we should have as full and unbroken an understanding as is possible between both Governments and peoples.

The London *Daily Mail*, a Conservative organ, in speaking of the Balfour Mission, published this strong editorial. If Mr. Balfour had done nothing else, he should feel proud to have evoked such words after his American visit:

The conclusion of Mr. Balfour's Mission to the United States has been marked in influential circles in America by tributes as warm as they are authoritative to the unqualified success the Foreign Secretary and his colleagues have achieved in their important and often delicate discussions with the administrative officials of the United States. We are rightly told little more than generalities as to the contribution America is making to the resources of the Alliance, but enough is known to satisfy us that our latest Ally is already

doing far more than had ever been asked of her at this
early stage. Her destroyers are on the Irish coast pro-
tecting our commerce, her yards are working at full
pressure on new hulls to carry our food, her munition
factories are doing us such service that our own plans
for industrial expansion can be abandoned. She is
raising loans to supply her European Allies, she is lim-
iting her own consumption that she may have food to
export to them, she is equipping a division to go at
once as an advance guard to France, she is preparing to
reorganise the Russian railways, she announces that
special efforts are to be exerted to train aviators and
build machines, "to ensure the blinding of the German
batteries, and to prevent German aviators from conducting operations near the Allies' lines."

Invaluable as such assistance is, it is only the first
fruits. But even when in months to come the full tale
of America's material contribution is reckoned up it
will be found in all likelihood to constitute the lesser
part of her full service to the world. Mr. Balfour and
President Wilson, it is stated, engaged in formal discussions on the nature and basis of a post-war settlement. We need not scrutinise too closely the authority of the report which credits the two statesmen with
identical views on that all-important theme, for Mr.
Wilson's policy has been defined in unequivocal language, and we cannot doubt that the practical applica-
tion of his principles would fall along lines that
would commend themselves without reserve to the
British Foreign Secretary. That is a factor of high
importance in the evolution of the future world. The
ideals for which we are contending in this war pro-
voke no difference of opinion among Allies so long as
they remain mere abstract ideals. But—to take a sin-

gle ideal alone, the rights of nationalities, to which
our allegiance is pledged—we shall gravely deceive
ourselves if we suppose that a settlement on racial
lines in Austria-Hungary, or the Balkans, or Asia Mi-
nor, will create no heartburnings and impose no strain
on loyalties among the Allies now fighting with a single
spirit and a single purpose. We point the finger of
suspicion at no one of the nations now in alliance with
us. To us ourselves there will be strong temptations,
in this quarter of the globe or that, to forsake for our
own advantage that disinterested pursuit of an unself-
ish ideal which our statesmen have repeatedly laid
down as our guiding principle in the war. To a minor-
ity in our own nation, and to like minorities among
other Allied peoples, that temptation will make a
strong appeal. It is essential that it shall be resisted,
and no Power will do more to fortify the resistance
than America. Her aims are above suspicion. She
seeks no oversea empire. She has intervened in a
European conflict with reluctance. If it should prove
necessary that in the future she should guarantee solely
or jointly the autonomy of some imperilled nation she
will assume the responsibility only as an unwelcome
duty. A great nation entering the Alliance in such a
spirit makes a contribution that means more to the
world than even her guns or her navies or her men.

THE SPEECH BEFORE THE EMPIRE PARLIAMENTARY ASSOCIATION

Other English papers wrote with equal enthusiasm when they welcomed Balfour home. The
Times published a long account of a luncheon
tendered the former Prime Minister by the Em-

pire Parliamentary Association, of which Mr.
Balfour is the chairman of the United Kingdom
Branch, and Mr. Asquith, who presided, is the
vice-president.   After the latter had made a
speech of welcome, Mr. Balfour replied as follows:

I admit that I undertook the headship of the mission to the United States with the greatest reluctance
and the greatest diffidence. The reluctance had many
causes.   There was the ocean (laughter)—quite apart
from submarines.   Measured in the true proportions
of terror, in fact, I should regard the submarine as the
least possible evil that could affect me.   (Laughter.)
But Providence was kind from the beginning to the end
of the mission, and the journey both ways across the
Atlantic was performed under the happiest auspices,
both of weather and everything else.   The diffidence
which I felt, however, had a deeper root even than the
hatred of the sea.   I felt it was very easy to do harm
and not very easy to do good.   On the whole, looking
back I feel that no harm was done and that much good
was accomplished.   (Cheers.)   If I may say so in the
absence of my colleagues in the mission, they performed their different tasks with admirable discretion,
great energy, and a full appreciation of all that is involved in the complex operation of bringing together
the effective forces of two great communities like Britain and the United States.   Do not let anybody suppose for a moment that the success of the mission was
due to the personal qualifications, whatever they may
have been, of the members of the mission.   It was
due to far greater, far deeper, and, I would fain hope

and believe, far more permanent causes than anything
purely personal could be.

The hospitality of the United States is proverbial,
and I do not dwell at this time, though I would gladly
do so on a fitting occasion, on the boundless hospitality
and kindness shown us both by the Central Government, by the State Governments, by the cities, and by
private individuals on the other side of the Atlantic.
That hospitality was limitless. It was not merely formal and external, but obviously it came from the heart,
and not one member of the mission will ever forget
all the kindness that was continually shown us from
the moment we crossed the frontier of the United
States. I think that hospitality would have been shown
whether the mission had been a success or whether it
had not been a success. I think the generous hospitality of our friends on the other side of the Atlantic
would have shown itself in any circumstances.

What moves me most, and what I think moves the
people in this country and in France, is something
much deeper than this kindly hospitality—the spon-
taneous exhibition of enthusiasm for the common
cause. This had nothing whatever to do with the personal qualifications or disqualifications of any individual. It had to do with the deeper feeling of sympathy
which manifestly animated the great American community from North to South and East to West. It
might have been in the power of emissaries who were
either unfortunate or indiscreet to check that manifes-
tation of feeling, but it was not in the power of individuals, however endowed, to create it. It did not
come from the mission. The mission was the occasion
of its exhibition and not the cause of the exhibition,
and that is the real value which has issued from any

such public efforts of the mission. The result of those efforts has been to give to the great American community the power of showing in the strongest, the most effective, and the most moving fashion what they felt of the great cause in which, as they knew, our Allies in France and we ourselves in this country have been engaged for nearly three years—the cause of world freedom. They knew the sacrifices that had been made and that were being made, they sympathised with the cause in which these sacrifices were undertaken, and when the moment came in which they felt bound to show on which side they stood they welcomed any opportunity of manifesting their deep moral and spiritual agreement with the policy which is being pursued by their present Allies on this side of the Atlantic. That is the real significance of the mission of which I was the head. That is the great result which it is having and has had—a result the value of which cannot be measured by its effect on this war, great as this effect is likely to be, but which will, I hope, outlast in the history of the world the life of even the youngest of those whom I am now addressing. I regard this mission not as the cause, but as the indication, of one of the most beneficent developments of international relations which has ever occurred in the history of the world. (Cheers.) Most alliances, as students of history know, are based upon the temporary hopes and temporary agreements of aim between nations which join together each for its own purpose, and whose alliance lasts only so long as the same end benefits both countries. Such alliances are inevitably doomed. They are based upon temporary necessities, and when the occasion is over they vanish, leaving behind, it may be, friendly or unfriendly relations, but not leaving be-

hind anything necessarily as a permanent basis. I
hope, and I believe, that the co-operation in this war
between Great Britain and America is not based upon
the fact that each has something to get out of the war
for itself, but is based upon a deep congruity and harmony of moral feeling and moral ideals. That is its
origin, and so also will be its history. It will endure
as long as our two nations are content to pursue these
great ideals, and I pray God it may be forever.
(Cheers.)

You may perhaps think I am drifting somewhat
away from the subject of the great struggle in which
we are all engaged. But, believe me, the considerations
I have been bringing to your notice have, in fact, reference, and an immense importance, in connexion with
the present struggle. As our alliance and co-operation
with the United States are based upon these great
moral considerations, and not upon any desire of this
country or of the United States to use the war as an
instrument of expansion, so we may be quite certain
that, as the United States have gone in with us for
these great ends, they will never leave us till these great
ends are accomplished. (Cheers.) There is nothing
of which I am more certain than this—the United
State, having put their hand to the plough, are not going to turn back. They watched the course of events
from the inception of this terrible war in August, 1914,
and, having studied the history which had led up to it,
having carefully contemplated the whole play of international forces in recent years, they have come to the
conclusion that with the victory of the Allies is bound
up the future of civilisation, as they and as we con-
ceive it. It is a conflict between two ideals, both of
which profess to be civilised—the German ideal, and

what, at all events in this connexion, I may call the
Anglo-Saxon ideal. They are clear, as we are clear,
that it is the second ideal which should regulate our
policy, and they are not going to abandon any effort,
or to refuse any sacrifice, any more than we are going
to abandon any effort, or refuse any sacrifice, which
may bring to a happy fruition a policy on which we are
all convinced depends not only immediate prosperity
for us and our children, but the whole trend of international and civilised evolution, as far as human eyes
and human powers of foresight can venture to pene-
trate the future. These are not the fruits of the mission, but I think the mission gave an occasion for the
emphatic expression of them, and if that be valuable,
and surely it is valuable, then we who took part in that
mission may congratulate ourselves on its result.
(Cheers.)

Who can doubt that Balfour came—and conquered!

THE END

Breinigsville, PA USA
28 July 2010
242645BV00001B/3/P